M000113298

The Plan

The Gospel Coalition Booklets

Edited by D. A. Carson & Timothy Keller

Gospel-Centered Ministry *by D. A. Carson and Timothy Keller*

The Restoration of All Things *by Sam Storms*

The Church: God's New People *by Tim Savage*

Creation *by Andrew M. Davis*

The Holy Spirit *by Kevin L. DeYoung*

Can We Know the Truth? *by Richard D. Phillips*

What Is the Gospel? *by Bryan Chapell*

The Plan

Colin S. Smith

CROSSWAY
WHEATON, ILLINOIS

The Plan

Published by Crossway
1300 Crescent Street
Wheaton, Illinois 60187

Cover design: Matthew Wahl

First printing 2011

Printed in the United States of America

All emphases in Scripture have been added by the author.

Trade paperback ISBN: 978-1-4335-2775-3

PDF ISBN: 978-1-4335-2776-0

Mobipocket ISBN: 978-1-4335-2777-7

ePub ISBN: 978-1-4335-2778-4

Crossway is a publishing ministry of Good News Publishers.

VP 20 19 18 17 16 15 14 13 12 11
14 13 12 11 10 9 8 7 6 5 4 3 2

Contents

Some people have the idea that God had a marvelous plan for the world but that things went terribly wrong and God had to come up with a costly initiative to sort out the mess. This is not what the Bible teaches.

God is not like the government, responding to unforeseen circumstances and making adjustments for unintended consequences. He is not like a scientist, experimenting to see what works, or a business entrepreneur who succeeds by finding new ideas that respond to emerging needs.

Bringing sinners to eternal life through Christ has always been God's plan. God promised eternal life "before the beginning of time, and at his appointed season he brought his word to light" (Titus 1:2–3). Before he created the world, God saw the joy that would come from redeeming a vast company of sinners from every circumstance of life, every continent of the world, and every generation of history. And knowing the cost, he determined to do it.

This is why the Bible describes Christ as "the Lamb that was slain from the creation of the world" (Rev. 13:8). Christ's death on the cross was not something that God came up with in response to Satan's triumph in the garden of Eden or as a last resort when it became evident that men and women couldn't live up to the Ten Commandments. Redeeming sinners from all nations through Jesus Christ was God's plan from the beginning.

God's plan is very different from our plans. When I say, "I'll meet you for breakfast next Tuesday," I mean, "Assuming that I'm alive, that I have transportation, that I don't have some other emergency, and that the restaurant is open and serving breakfast, I will see you on Tuesday."

Our plans are contingent. They depend on how events unfold and whether we have the ability to bring them about. Many things in life are beyond our control.

But God is sovereign. He fulfills his own plan in his own time by his own power, and no one can stop him. God knows exactly what he is doing at every point in history in every nation of the world and through every event in your life.

This should be a great comfort to you. Nothing you have ever done has taken God by surprise. Nothing that has happened to you has caught him unaware. Nothing you do and nothing that happens to you can stop God from fulfilling his plan or even slow him down. That is what it means for God to be sovereign.

God knows exactly what he is doing. You can have confidence in knowing that the events of your life are not spinning out of control or settled by random chance but that they are in the hands of God, who plans for you in love. Christians find joy in knowing that God's plan will lead to the greatest possible display of his glory and the greatest possible joy for his people.

I invite you to join me on a whistle-stop tour through the Bible's storyline, where God reveals the splendor of his breathtaking purpose that sweeps from eternity past through the ages of human history into eternity future.

We begin with the Old Testament, where God lays out the blueprints for his plan. Then, in the Gospels, we look at how Jesus Christ achieves all that is needed for the plan to be accomplished. And finally we look at the New Testament letters and rejoice in how the Holy Spirit delivers all that God has promised and all that Christ has accomplished in the lives of all God's people.

God Makes a Promise: The Story of the Old Testament

God unfolds his plan through seven initiatives that are full of promise for all his people.

Creation

"In the beginning God created the heavens and the earth" (Gen. 1:1). Try to imagine nothing. It's almost impossible! But before the creation there was nothing, except God. God created all things, and all things belong to him. "The earth is the LORD's and everything in it, the world, and all who live in it" (Ps. 24:1).

Take a fresh look at what God has created today. Look at the sky; it proclaims the work of God's hands. Listen to the birds; they testify to God's gentle care. Every snowflake bears witness to his majesty. Every sunrise speaks of his faithfulness. "The heavens declare the glory of God; the skies proclaim the work of his hands. . . . There is no speech or language where their voice is not heard" (Ps. 19:1–3).

The whole creation reflects the glory of God, but God did something of a different order when he made the first man and woman. We know this because God said, "Let us make man in our image, in our likeness, and let them rule over the fish of the sea and the birds of the air, over the livestock, over all the earth, and over all the creatures that move along the ground" (Gen. 1:26).

God made the man and the woman in his image. This is why you are different from a plant, an animal, a fish, or a bird. They were all made *by* God, but only humans were made *like* God. That gives human life unique value.

God chose to bring you into being. He has never made anyone quite like you before, and he will never make anyone quite like you again. You are not an accident. Your life is not a product of random chance. You were made by God, and you were made for God. The ultimate purpose of your life is that you should radiate a unique reflection of Jesus Christ. You were made to glorify God and to enjoy him forever.

What does God promise? *God promises to give life to people who reflect his glory.*

The Bible never fully explains the origin of evil; it simply tells us that God placed the man and the woman in a garden where everything was good. Their food was provided on the trees; their work was fulfilling; their union and joy in marriage was complete; and they lived in fellowship with God, who appeared to them and walked with them in the garden.

There was a tree in the garden called "the tree of the knowledge of good and evil," and God told the man and the woman not to eat from the tree (Gen. 2:17). Since everything they knew was good, the only thing they could gain by disobeying God was the knowledge of evil.

A serpent came enticing them with the knowledge of evil, and that is what they chose. In the act of disobeying God, they got the knowledge of evil, and we have all been stuck with it ever since. But God took the initiative and made another promise.

Destruction

God said to the Serpent, "Cursed are you" (Gen. 3:14). To curse means to assign to destruction. God was saying to the Serpent, "What you have done will not stand. You will be destroyed, and all that is evil will be destroyed with you." God's curse on the Serpent opens the door of hope for us.

Then God said to Adam, "Cursed is the ground because of you" (Gen. 3:17). The ground hadn't done anything wrong! Adam deserved the curse because of his sin. But God diverted the curse away from the man and woman and onto the ground so that instead of being destroyed with the Serpent, they might be reconciled to him.

What does God promise? *God promises to destroy evil and rid the world of its curse.*

How would this happen? God said to the Evil One, "I will put enmity between you and the woman, and between your offspring and hers; he will crush your head, and you will strike his heel" (Gen. 3:15).

The human race would always be in conflict with evil. That has proved true for every person in every culture in every generation. But God speaks of an offspring, someone who will come into the line of human history, born of the woman. He will be on our side. He will stand with us in this great conflict and act for us against all the powers of evil. Satan will strike his heel, but even as the Serpent bites his feet, our Champion will crush the serpent's head.

Life continued for Adam and Eve outside the garden of Eden. God's grace had saved them from immediate judgment and given them the hope of eventual restoration, but they soon discovered that the evil unleashed through their disobedience brought devastating changes within them and around them.

The first human family was torn apart when Cain murdered his brother Abel and then spent the rest of his life in fear that his deed would be avenged (Genesis 4). The knowledge of evil was already proving a liability. It had already separated the man and the woman from God. Now it was tearing up a family.

As violence increased, people came together to build a city, hoping that collective security would be the answer (Genesis 11). But what started with great hope ended in disappointment as people dispersed to the north, south, east, and west, driven by fear and divided by language.

Then out of all the emerging tribes and nations of the world, God chose one man.

Election

"I will bless you . . . and you will be a blessing . . . . All peoples on earth will be blessed through you" (Gen. 12:2–3). Abraham knew absolutely nothing about God. He was an idolater, living in complete spiritual darkness (Josh. 24:2). But God swept into his life uninvited and changed him forever.

If God waited for you or for me to seek after him, he would still be waiting. No one seeks God (Rom. 3:11). No one! By nature we run from God. If we seek him, it is because he has taken the initiative to seek us and to draw us to himself.

God made it clear to Abraham that this was precisely what he intended to do in the lives of people from every nation on the planet. God would gather a people from every race and language, every level of education and income, and bring them into the full knowledge of his blessing.

What is God promising now? *God promises to bless people from all nations.*

This blessing would not come to people from all nations through Abraham himself or through his descendants in general, but through one child called "the seed," who would be born into Abraham's line (Gal. 3:16). That is why the Old Testament follows the story of Abraham's descendants.

Abraham and Sarah were getting old, and they had no children. But through a miracle of God's grace, Sarah conceived in her old age and gave birth to a son, Isaac. Isaac's son, Jacob, had twelve sons who became the fathers of the twelve tribes of Israel.

God cared for this extended family in a special way. When famine threatened their lives, God provided food for them in Egypt. In the years that followed God blessed them by multiplying their number so that the extended family of about seventy grew to a community of about two million people over a period of about four hundred years.

God's people were despised as they grew in number. They were treated with great cruelty and became slaves in Egypt. But God saw their suffering and had compassion on them.

Redemption

"The LORD said, 'I have indeed seen the misery of my people in Egypt. . . . So I have come down to rescue them . . . and to bring them . . . [into] a land flowing with milk and honey'" (Ex. 3:7–8). God raised up a man called Moses and sent him to Egypt's pagan king with this command: "Let my people go" (Ex. 5:1). The king did not recognize God's authority, so he refused God's command and came under his judgment. God sent a series of plagues that led to a devastating judgment in which death came across the whole land.

Before God sent this judgment, he gave his people a command and a promise: each family was to slaughter a lamb and take the blood and paint it on their doorframe to indicate that death had already come to their house (Ex. 12:7). Then God said, "When I see the blood, I will pass over you" (Ex. 12:13).

On the night of the Passover, God's sacrifice brought his people out of slavery and delivered them from his judgment. After this, God made a covenant with them: "I will walk among you and be your God, and you will be my people" (Lev. 26:12).

God gave his people commandments and sacrifices. We need the commandments because God calls his people to walk in his ways. Those who bear his name must reflect his character. But God's people need more than commands. We need the sacrifices, because at our best we are still sinners who fall far short of the glory of God.

God's people had been delivered from judgment by the blood of a slaughtered lamb. In the same way, their fellowship with God would be sustained through a sacrifice offered for their sins. What is God promising now? *God promises to reconcile sinners to himself through a sacrifice.*

God's people were not satisfied with this arrangement—they wanted a king. God gave them the kind of king they wanted, and he turned out to be a disaster. Then God gave them another king, and to this man God gave an extraordinary promise.

Dominion

"I will raise up your offspring to succeed you, who will come from your own body, and I will establish his kingdom. He is the one who will build a house for my Name, and I will establish the throne of his kingdom forever" (2 Sam. 7:12–13).

God's people had a taste of his blessing in the time of King David that surpassed anything they had known before. With their enemies subdued and their borders secure, God's people prospered. But what would happen after David?

Every father wants the best for his son, so God had David's attention when he spoke about David's offspring: God promised to raise up David's own son and establish his kingdom. David's son would fulfill David's dream to build a house for God's name.

Then God gave a promise so great that David had to sit down to take it in. God promised to establish the kingdom of David's son *forever*, and he said, "I will be his father and he will be my son" (2 Sam. 7:14). The first son in view is David's immediate son Solomon, who follows his father to the throne. But the promise of an eternal dynasty of David (2 Sam. 7:16) anticipates a son who will outstrip both David and Solomon. How can any kingdom last forever? And in what sense will this son of David also be the Son of God?

As we travel through the Old Testament story, we're building a picture of God's plan and of the person who will deliver what God promises: to give life to people who will reflect his glory, to destroy evil and rid the world of its curse, to bless people from all nations, and to reconcile sinners to himself through a sacrifice for sins.

The one who fulfills this promise will be born of a woman; he will be the seed of Abraham and a descendent of David, a king who will bring the blessing of God's rule. God will be his Father, and he will be God's Son. God will establish the throne of his kingdom forever. What is God promising now? *God promises that his people will live under the blessing of his rule forever.*

After David there followed a line of kings; some were good, but most were bad. God's people worshiped other gods and walked in their ways. God sent messengers called "prophets" to call his people back to obedience. Their message was largely ignored. So God, whose word never fails, moved to discipline and correct his people.

Correction

"This is what the Lord says: 'When seventy years are completed for Babylon, I will come to you and fulfill my gracious promise to bring you back to this place. For I know the plans I have for you,' declares the Lord, 'plans to prosper you and not to harm you, plans to give you hope and a future'" (Jer. 29:10–11).

The land God had given to his people was overrun by enemies, and God's people became exiles. They lived in Babylon under the discipline of God and wept their way through seventy years of sorrow and repentance.

But even in this most severe discipline, God was advancing his purpose for his people. God receives us in our sin, but he never leaves us in our sins. He is relentless in calling us to follow his ways and in correcting us when we depart from them. What is God promising now? *God promises that all his people will walk in all his ways.*

When God's redeeming work in your life is complete, you will love God with all your heart, mind, soul, and strength, you will love your neighbor as yourself, and you will share the joy of this love with all the people of God forever.

Until that day, God will not rest content where his people cling to sins that he has clearly told us to forsake. God is not in the business of ferrying unchanged, self-centered sinners into the joys of eternal life. God calls us to obedience, and when we resist his call, we should expect to come under his loving discipline that refuses to let us go.

After seventy years, God brought his chastened people back to the Promised Land. This restoration was a miracle of God's grace that had seemed impossible. But then God gave one man a vision of what he was about to do.

Restoration

"Son of man, these bones are the whole house of Israel. They say, 'Our bones are dried up and our hope is gone; we are cut off.' Therefore prophesy and say to them: 'This is what the Sovereign LORD says: O my people, I am going to open your graves and bring you up from them; I will bring you back to the land of Israel. Then you, my people, will know that I am the LORD'" (Ezek. 37:11–13).

God's promises are so great that faith staggers before them. That's how it was for God's people in the time of Ezekiel. Jerusalem lay in ruins; most of its people had fled or died; and those who survived were exiles in Babylon under a regime that had no intention of letting them go.

God's people knew his promises, but the destruction of evil, God's blessing on all nations, and the joys of the Davidic kingdom seemed like another world from their daily grind. God's people found it hard to sing his praises in this strange land.

Then God gave the prophet Ezekiel a vision in which he saw a valley of dry bones. This picture fitted the mood of God's people, who were saying, "Our bones are dried up and our hope is gone; we are cut off" (Ezek. 37:11). They had come to feel that their situation was hopeless.

In the vision, Ezekiel spoke God's word to the bones, and as he did, the bones came together. Then they were covered with tendons, flesh, and skin, and the Spirit of God breathed life into the corpses, just as he had breathed life into Adam. God was bringing new life from the grave. What is God promising now? *God promises new life from the grave.*

Conclusion

The Old Testament is the story of God's amazing promises. Step back and try to take it in:

1) God promises to give life to people who will reflect his glory.
2) God promises to destroy evil and rid the world of its curse.
3) God promises to bless people from all nations.
4) God promises to reconcile sinners to himself through a sacrifice for sins.
5) God promises that his people will live under the blessing of his rule forever.
6) God promises that all his people will walk in all his ways.
7) God promises to bring new life from the grave.

By any standard, these are amazing promises. Only God could make them, and only God can fulfill them. To find out how he has done that and to see what these promises can mean for you, we turn to the New Testament.

Christ Fulfills the Promise: The Story of the Gospels

God makes promises so great that only God himself could deliver them, so God took human flesh in Jesus Christ. The Creator entered his own creation. God came and stood with us, acting for us, to fulfill his own promise. The Word who was with God and was God and by whom all things were made became flesh and made his dwelling among us (John 1:2, 14). The Gospels tell us what Jesus Christ has accomplished for his people.

Incarnation

"The angel answered, 'The Holy Spirit will come upon you, and the power of the Most High will overshadow you. So the holy one to be born will be called the Son of God'" (Luke 1:35).

The angel announced to Mary that Jesus would be "the Son of the Most High" and "the Son of God" (Luke 1:32, 35), and Matthew records that he is "God with us" (Matt 1:23). John describes him as the "Word [who] became flesh" (John 1:14).

God spoke his promise in words. Then when his Word became flesh, God's promise was delivered. Only God can deliver what God has promised. That is why Christian praise and thanksgiving are so intimately tied up with the confession that Jesus Christ is God and that Jesus Christ is a human being. As we are born, so also was Christ born—to live our life and to die our death. He came to us and stands with us to act for us. As God, he delivers what God has promised; as man, he delivers what God has promised to us.

The angel also announced that Jesus is holy: "the holy one" (Luke 1:35). Here's something that has never been seen before in the history of the world, nor will it ever be seen again: a *man* who is holy by nature. This man belongs in heaven by right and, because he is God, has the capacity to bring others there with him.

The union of God and man in Jesus Christ, the Holy One, opens the door of hope for us. John Calvin says this beautifully:

> In short, since neither as God alone could he feel death, nor as man alone could he overcome it, he coupled human nature with divine that to atone for sin he might submit the weakness of the one to death; and that, wrestling with death by the power of the other nature, he might win victory for us.[1]

This is the purpose of the incarnation. Only the God-man could deliver the promises of God to men and women. The birth of the Holy One of God led to the perfect, sinless life of our Lord Jesus Christ.

Temptation

"Jesus, full of the Holy Spirit, returned from the Jordan and was led by the Spirit in the desert, where for forty days he was tempted by the devil" (Luke 4:1–2). Christ confronted Satan when he was led by the Spirit to be tempted by Satan, and Christ triumphed where Adam failed. The Serpent tempted Jesus three times, just as he had done with Eve and Adam. The parallels are obvious, but we must not miss the differences.

The environment was clearly different. Eve and Adam faced temptation in a garden with food supplied on the trees all around them. Christ faced temptation in a desert where there was no food, and he was hungry.

The initiatives were different. Satan came looking for the woman in the garden. But Christ went after Satan in the desert. The Holy Spirit led him into confrontation with the Devil. Christ stalked Satan, drew him out into the open, and initiated the confrontation.

The greatest difference was the outcome. Where Adam failed, Christ triumphed. Having plied Christ with his most exquisite temptation, Satan was forced to retreat "until an opportune time" (Luke 4:13). Overcoming the Holy One by temptation was clearly not an option.

Christ's triumph over temptation has huge significance for us. Adam's failure brought misery for us. He passed on the effects of his failure to all who derive their life from him. By nature we belong to Adam, who failed. We share in his failure. We are "under sin" (Rom. 3:9).

But Christ's triumph brings hope for us. As Adam passed on the effects of his failure to all who derive their life from him, so Christ passes on the effects of his triumph to all who draw *new life* from him. By grace and through faith we belong to Christ who triumphed. We share in his triumph. We are "under grace" (Rom. 6:14).

The weakness of Adam, who failed, is in you, so be on your guard against temptation. But the strength of Christ, who triumphed, is also in you by the Holy Spirit, so when we are tempted, we can stand firm.

After his triumph in the desert, "Jesus returned to Galilee in the power of the Spirit, and news about him spread through the whole countryside" (Luke 4:14). What happened next will help you to understand our experience of life in the world today.

Rejection

"'The Spirit of the Lord is on me, because he has anointed me to preach good news to the poor. He has sent me to proclaim freedom for the prisoners and recovery of sight for the blind, to release the oppressed, to proclaim the year of the Lord's favor.' . . . All the people in the synagogue were furious when they heard this" (Luke 4:18–19, 28).

Picture the small crowd gathered in the synagogue as Jesus reads the Scripture and explains its meaning. His words are full of hope, but the people respond not with joy but with fury. They were "furious." In some circles of the ministry of Jesus Christ, who comes to our aid, he was rejected from the beginning, and this theme runs right through the Gospels.

On another occasion, Jesus healed a man whose hand was paralyzed. It was an amazing miracle, but notice the response: the Pharisees "were furious and began to discuss with one another what they might do to Jesus" (Luke 6:11). Another time Christ cast demons out of a man who had terrorized his community with violence. But when the people saw the man who had plagued them sitting dressed and in his right mind, they asked Jesus to leave the region (Luke 8:37).

This pattern of rejection culminated in the crowd calling for Jesus to be crucified. Pilate tried to intervene, but "with loud shouts they insistently demanded that he be crucified, and their shouts prevailed" (Luke 23:23).

We live in a Christ-rejecting world. You cannot understand the world in which we live until you grasp this: Christ "came to that which was his own, but his own did not receive him" (John 1:11).

When natural disasters happen, people ask, "Why doesn't God do something about that?" But when he came and calmed the storm, we rejected him. When gunmen terrorize schools, we ask, "Why doesn't God do something about that?" But when he came and cast out demons, we asked him to leave. When cancer comes we ask, "Why doesn't God do something about that?" But when he came and healed the sick, people rejected him.

"He came to his own and his own did not receive him." Thank God it doesn't end there. "*Yet* to all who received him . . . he gave the right to become children of God" (John 1:12).

Here's our position as Christians: we live in a Christ-rejecting world with all its sin and death, but we belong to a Christ-exalting family with all its life and joy. We experience *both* the pain of this fallen world *and* the hope of all who are in Christ *at the same time*.

While the world was rejecting him, Jesus went up a mountain with three of his disciples.

Transfiguration

"As he was praying, the appearance of his face changed, and his clothes became as bright as a flash of lightning" (Luke 9:29). Peter, James, and John saw the glory, brightness, and splendor of Jesus Christ. They saw what the angels see in heaven and what one day every human eye will see. How bright is a flash of lightning? Jesus, whom these men had come to know as a friend, was and is the brightness of the Father's glory (Heb. 1:3).

But there's more: "Two men, Moses and Elijah, appeared in glorious splendor, talking with Jesus" (Luke 9:30–31). Moses and Elijah had lived and died hundreds of years before. Now they appear, large-as-life, sharing the glory of Jesus.

Then the voice of the Almighty spoke from the cloud saying, "This is my Son, whom I have chosen; listen to him" (Luke 9:35). The world today rejects Christ. But God calls you to listen to him. God has chosen him, and he is able to bring dead men into glory!

The disciples did not stay on the mountain. The cloud vanished; Moses and Elijah disappeared from view; and Jesus' face became as they had known it before. The disciples had to live by faith, just as we do, and when they came down the mountain, they walked back into a world filled with great evil and profound need.

Crucifixion

"When they came to the place called the Skull, there they crucified him" (Luke 23:33). Our sin reached its full horror and found its most awful expression in the cross. We all disobeyed God's commands; then we crucified God's Son. God's judgment had to fall on the human race, but God diverted the judgment we deserve to another place.

As the soldiers were nailing Jesus to the cross, our Lord prayed, "Father, forgive them, for they do not know what they are doing" (Luke 23:34). When Jesus said this, he was isolating himself under the judgment of God. He knew that judgment would come that day, and it did. But he cried out to the Father, "Don't let it come on them. Let it fall on me."

That is what happened at Calvary. The punishment due to your sin was poured out on Jesus. Christ became the lightning rod for your judgment, and forgiveness was released through his suffering and death on the cross for you. The curse fell on Jesus because he "bore our sins" (1 Pet. 2:24). The weight of our guilt was "laid on him" (Isa. 53:6), and he became the sacrifice for our sins.

Christ's death changes death for all his people. When you die, you will not carry your sin and guilt into *your* death because he carried it into *his* death for you. If you are in Christ, you will never know what it is like to die a sin-bearing death.

When our sin reached its full horror, God's love was displayed in all its glory. If you doubt God's love for you, look at the cross. No other love can match this. Nothing else in our experience can come close. God's love for us in Christ is greater than we ever dared to dream.

Resurrection

"He is not here. He has risen!" (Luke 24:6). On Easter morning a group of women went to the tomb where the body of Jesus had been laid and found it empty. The good news that they heard was not "Jesus is alive" but "He has risen." The Son of God was alive in heaven before he took human flesh. He could have returned to heaven, leaving his crucified body in the tomb. The angels could have said, "His body is in the tomb, but don't be afraid; his Spirit is with the Father in heaven." But that would not have fulfilled God's plan of redemption for us.

When God created the angels, he made them souls without bodies, and when he created animals, he made them bodies without souls. But he created us as a unique integration of body and soul together.

Death separates what God has joined. It is the undoing of our nature, and that is why death is such a terrible enemy. But Christ went through death, triumphed over death, and came out of death. He came to redeem your life—soul and body—and to present all of you, without fault and with great joy, to your Father in heaven (Jude 24).

Then Christ opened the minds of the disciples so they could see that the whole message of the Bible leads to and flows from his death and resurrection. He told them, "The Christ will suffer and rise from the dead on the third day, and repentance and forgiveness of sins will be preached in his name to all nations" (Luke 24:46–47).

Christ was crystal-clear about the message the apostles were to preach: repentance and forgiveness of sins. Repentance means that you completely change your mind about your sin and your whole position toward Jesus Christ. You separate yourself from the world's rejection of Jesus, and you take your stand with him, trusting in his mercy and placing yourself under his authority.

Forgiveness means that Jesus Christ embraces you in love. He cleanses your guilt, reconciles you to God the Father, and enters your life through his Spirit—giving you power to live the new life of faith and the obedience to which he calls you.

Ascension

"He lifted up his hands and blessed them. While he was blessing them, he left them and was taken up into heaven" (Luke 24:50–51). The last glimpse the disciples had of Jesus was with his hands raised, blessing them. Christ's atoning work on the cross was finished. But his work of blessing the disciples continued even as he ascended into heaven. This wonderful reality must have been sealed in their minds and hearts by the manner of Christ's ascension.

Today at the right hand of the Father, Christ continues to bless his people. His hands are not raised against us, but for us. He does not speak condemnation to us but blessing. His words are life. When you are "in Christ," everything that is his becomes yours. His sin-bearing death is yours, his resurrection life is yours, and one day you will share in his ascension too.

> The Lord himself will come down from heaven, with a loud command, with the voice of the archangel and with the trumpet call of God, and the dead in Christ [i.e., believers who have passed through death into the presence of Jesus] will rise first. After that, we who are still alive . . . will be caught up together with them . . . to meet the Lord in the air. (1 Thess. 4:16–17)

When Christ comes in glory, all his people will share in his ascension. The bodies of those who have died will be raised. The bodies of those who are still alive will be changed, and God's people, redeemed in Christ, will be with him forever.

Conclusion

Here is the breathtaking sweep of what God promises us in Jesus Christ. Jesus came and lived and died and rose again so that:

1) We might become a new creation fully reflecting the image of God.
2) We might be delivered from the curse of evil.
3) We might enjoy the blessing of God together with a vast company of redeemed people from all nations.

4) We might be reconciled to God through Christ, who offered himself as the sacrifice for our sins.
5) We might live under the blessing of God's rule forever.
6) We might walk in God's ways, loving him with all our heart and our neighbor as ourselves.
7) We might receive new life from the grave.

God seals all his promises with his own "yes" in Jesus (2 Cor. 1:20). Jesus is the green light on all of God's promises, and you can have full confidence that everything God has promised is yours in him.

Next we turn to the New Testament letters, where we see how the Holy Spirit applies all that Christ has accomplished in the lives of his people.

The Church Communicates the Promise: The Story of the Acts

Before Jesus ascended into heaven, he promised to send the Holy Spirit to his disciples. Christ was returning to the Father in heaven, but his presence and power would be with them and in them by the Holy Spirit.

Christ's promise was fulfilled on the day of Pentecost. Peter spoke to a large crowd of people from all nations gathered in Jerusalem. He described the life, death, and resurrection of Jesus, and then, filled with the Holy Spirit, he declared, "God has made this Jesus, whom you crucified, both Lord and Christ" (Acts 2:36).

The people clearly believed what Peter was telling them. If they didn't, they would have argued or simply walked away. But that was not their reaction. "When the people heard this [i.e., Peter's message about Jesus], they were cut to the heart and said to Peter and the other apostles, 'Brothers, what shall we do?'" (Acts 2:37).

Peter replied, "Repent" (Acts 2:38). That's important. True faith is shot through with repentance, and true repentance is shot through with faith. Faith and repentance are like two sides of a coin; you can't have one without the other. Faith and repentance are birthed together when you see the love and mercy of God for you in Jesus Christ.

Peter continued, "Repent and be baptized, every one of you, in the name of Jesus Christ" (Acts 2:38). Peter tells them to publicly identify themselves with the Lord Jesus Christ and receive the mark, the sign, the seal, of God's promise. God promises the forgiveness of sins and the gift of the Holy Spirit to everyone he calls (Acts 2:38–39). God will forgive you. He will reconcile you to himself. Christ will give you new life by the Holy Spirit, whom he will give to you.

It's worth remembering that Peter was speaking in the same city where Jesus had been crucified just fifty days earlier. Some who were there on the day of Pentecost would also have been in the crowd that called for him to be crucified, crying, "Let his blood be on us and on our children" (Matt. 27:25); it is to *these people* that Peter speaks about Christ's forgiveness and the gift of his Holy Spirit: "The promise is for you and your children and for all who are far off—for all whom the Lord our God will call" (Acts 2:39).

The promise is for "you." If you believe in the Lord Jesus Christ and turn from your sin, God will forgive you for all that you have done. He will give you his Holy Spirit, making it possible for you to break free from old ways and live a new life.

The promise is for "your children." That means it is not limited to one generation that lived two thousand years ago. It is not locked in the past. This promise is never outdated. It spans the centuries, and it is for us today.

The promise is for all who are "far off." The promise of forgiveness and new life in Jesus Christ is for people from every background. If you feel far from God today, this promise is for you.

God promised that through the seed of Abraham, people from every nation on earth would be blessed. Forgiveness and new life in Jesus Christ is God's promise for people in Africa, Asia, the Americas, Europe, Australia, and Antarctica. The mission of the church is to take this good news of Jesus Christ to every person.

The promise is for "all whom the Lord our God will call." He calls through the gospel. God was calling those people right there, as Peter was speaking about Christ. God is calling you today, as you read the good news of the gospel. There is forgiveness and new life for you in Jesus Christ today.

The Holy Spirit Delivers the Promise: The Story of the New Testament Letters

What does this new life in Christ look like? What happens when the Holy Spirit delivers God's promise in a person who repents and believes? What has God done for you and in you through Jesus Christ?

The New Testament letters take us inside God's promise to show us all that is ours in Jesus Christ. I want you to see the sweep of God's redeeming work in a human life. It begins with regeneration.

Regeneration: You Have New Life

"Praise be to the God and Father of our Lord Jesus Christ! In his great mercy he has given us new birth into a living hope through the resurrection of Jesus Christ from the dead. . . . For you have been born again, not of perishable seed, but of imperishable, through the living and enduring word of God" (1 Pet. 1:3, 23).

When God created the heavens and the earth, our planet was formless and empty—a dark, watery chaos. The Spirit of God hovered over the waters (Gen. 1:2); then God spoke light into darkness and brought life to the world. God formed the beauty of the earth.

The same Spirit who hovered over the waters at creation is like a wind blowing into human lives (John 3:8). He gives light to people who cannot see Christ's glory (2 Cor. 4:4), and he brings new life to people who are dead toward God (Eph. 2:1).

Jesus says, "The Spirit gives birth to spirit" (John 3:6). When the Holy Spirit regenerates you, he changes your soul so that with a new mind and a new heart you love Christ, trust him, and follow him freely. Jesus describes this miracle as being "born again" or "born of the Spirit" (John 3:7–8). Behind all believing lies this miracle of God's regenerating grace.

The interface of regeneration and faith is a mystery that should lead you to worship. God's children are known and distinguished by faith in the Lord Jesus Christ. "To all who received him, to those who *believed* in his name, he gave the right to become children of God" (John 1:12).

But why have you believed when others have not? Why did you come to faith when you did and not before or after? God took the initiative in regenerating you. God opened your eyes to see the glory of Christ. The Holy Spirit hovered over the dark chaos of your life and made you a new creation in Christ.

Do you see that God has done something amazing in your soul, giving you new life from above? God has given you a new heart. He has put his Spirit in you. He has given you new birth into a living hope through the resurrection of Jesus Christ from the dead (1 Pet. 1:3).

Union: You Are in Christ

"Don't you know that all of us who were baptized into Christ Jesus were baptized into his death? We were therefore buried with him through baptism into death in order that, just as Christ was raised from the dead through the glory of the Father, we too may live a new life" (Rom. 6:3–4)

When I baptize people, I plunge them down into the water. When a person is baptized in the Holy Spirit, he or she is plunged "into the Spirit," and is thus united with Christ. This union with Christ is the wonderful reality to which baptism in water points.

Taking his cue from the New Testament, Martin Luther describes the believer's union with Christ using the analogy of marriage:

> Faith . . . unites the soul to Christ as a bride is united with her bridegroom. By this mystery, as the Apostle teaches, Christ and the soul become one flesh. And if they are one flesh and there is between them a true marriage . . . it follows that everything they have, they hold in common. . . . Accordingly the believing soul can boast of and glory in whatever Christ has as though it were its own.[2]

I was thinking recently about folks in the church we served in England and how little I have done to keep in touch with them. I was also thinking about some other projects I'm behind on, and I was having an "O wretched man that I am" kind of day. The following morning, my wife, Karen, was sitting at our dining room table working on Christmas letters. She sends over one hundred cards to England—each one with a handwritten note—and she signs it: "From Karen *and Colin.*"

There I was, thinking about my wretched failure to keep in touch with these people, when actually I have written to them every year for the last fourteen years! In isolation I have done a wretched job, but when I see that I am united to my wife, I have joy because I share in what she has done. A letter has gone out in my name every year!

Christ has done for us what we have failed to do for ourselves. He has lived the life that we have not lived and cannot live. But when we are "in Christ," all that he has done is ours—his life, death, and resurrection have our name on them as though they were our own.

That's union with Christ. What it meant for him was being nailed to the cross. What it means for us is justification.

Justification: You Are Declared Righteous

"Therefore, since we have been justified through faith, we have peace with God through our Lord Jesus Christ" (Rom. 5:1). "Justified" is a legal word that describes a verdict. When God justifies, he pronounces a person righteous. When he condemns, he declares a person guilty. Justification and condemnation are about recognizing something that is already true.

When justice prevails, a guilty man will be sentenced and an innocent man will be acquitted. Being acquitted does not make a man innocent; it is the man's innocence that leads to him being acquitted. In the same way, being sentenced does not make a man a criminal; it is the man's crime that leads to him being sentenced.

As a matter of simple justice, we should expect God to condemn sinners and justify the righteous. But here is something truly amazing: God justifies *sinners*. Try to let that massive contradiction sink into your mind. God justifies *sinners!* How can he do that?

God presented Jesus as a propitiation for our sins (Rom. 3:25). That means when Jesus died, all the anger and hostility that God rightly has toward sin, wickedness, and evil was poured out on him. Like a cup filled with God's judgment, Jesus drank all of it until it was empty. At the cross Christ absorbed God's judgment that was due to our sin.

Faith unites us to Christ, and when we are "in Christ," God counts all our sin as his and all his righteousness as ours. He bore our condemnation, and we are justified in him. Through the cross, God demonstrated his justice so as to be just and at the same time the one who justifies those who have faith in Jesus (Rom. 3:26).

If God justified only the righteous, how could we have any hope? The good news is that God justifies the ungodly (Rom. 4:5). As faith unites us to Jesus Christ, the power of his atoning sacrifice becomes ours. We are freed from the fear of condemnation due to our sin and guilt and brought into his marvelous love.

Adoption: You Are Loved

"When the time had fully come, God sent his Son, born of a woman, born under law, to redeem those under law, that we might receive the full rights of sons. Because you are sons, God sent the Spirit of his Son into our hearts, the Spirit who calls out, '*Abba*, Father.' So you are no longer a slave, but a son; and since you are a son, God has made you also an heir" (Gal. 4:4–7).

Through Christ, God adopts us into his family and loves us as his own sons and daughters. No other experience of love can compare to the love God has for you in Christ. Someone may pledge to love us "as long as we both shall live," but God pledges his love to us in life, through death and for eternity. No one else can say to us, "Never will I leave you; never will I forsake you" (Heb. 13:5).

God loves us with an everlasting love. That means that God loved us before we were born and even before the creation of the world. Christ had us in view when he came into the world, when he hung on the cross, and when he rose from the dead.

It is the special work of the Holy Spirit to convince us that we are a dearly loved child of God. "God has poured out his love into our hearts by the Holy Spirit, whom he has given us" (Rom. 5:5). The Spirit makes God's love real in our experience. He connects us to the reality of God's love for us that was demonstrated conclusively at the cross.

One of the challenges you will face in the Christian life is to wean yourself off the habit of discerning God's love on the basis of feelings or circumstances. Our natural instinct is to feel that God loves us when we are healthy, have a good job, and life is going well. But when the wheels start to come off, our first instinct is to question God's love and assume the worst.

What we ought to do is remind ourselves of the incalculable demonstration of God's love in the cross. "He who did not spare his own Son, but gave him up for us all—how will he not also, along with him, graciously give us all things?" (Rom. 8:32).

Sanctification: You Will Be Holy

"May God himself, the God of peace, sanctify you through and through. May your whole spirit, soul and body be kept blameless at the coming of our Lord Jesus Christ. The one who calls you is faithful and he will do it" (1 Thess. 5:23–24).

Sanctification is the progressive work of the Holy Spirit in a believer by which we grow in the life God is calling us to live. It is the desire and longing of every Christian's heart. Bishop Ryle says:

> Most men hope to go to heaven when they die; but few, it may be feared, take the trouble to consider whether they would enjoy heaven if they got there. Heaven is essentially a holy place. . . . What could an unsanctified man do in heaven if by chance he got there?[3]

To paraphrase John Owen on this same point:

> There is no idea more foolish or pernicious than this—that a person who is not sanctified, not made holy in this life, should afterwards be taken into the blessedness that consists in the enjoyment of God. Such a person cannot enjoy God, nor would God be a reward to them. Holiness is perfected in heaven, but it is always begun in this world.[4]

Justification and sanctification are always found together in Christ, and grasping how they interrelate is crucial to understanding the gospel. The two most common errors are to confuse or separate them. Confusion happens if you slide into thinking that your standing with God depends in some way on your performance in the Christian life. It doesn't. You are justified by faith in the finished work of Christ.

Separation occurs when a Christian gets the idea that since we are justified by faith alone, obedience to Christ really doesn't matter. It does. Christ holds the blessings of justification and sanctification *in himself*. When we embrace Christ by faith, these gifts become ours together. Nobody has the one without the other.

That's why the Bible says, "Without holiness no one will see the Lord" (Heb. 12:14). This doesn't mean that we are saved by being holy but that the pursuit of holiness is evidence that we are in Christ, who justifies us by his blood.

Paul prays for the sanctification of believers, "May God himself, the God of peace, sanctify you through and through"—and we should pray for our sanctification too. But sanctification is also a promise: "The one who calls you is faithful and he will do it" (1 Thess. 5:24).

Hold on to that promise when you are discouraged over your lack of progress in the Christian life. What God's grace has begun in you will be completed for his glory and for your joy. God will give you the desire of your heart. You will be conformed to the likeness of his Son, forever (Rom. 8:29).

Glorification: You Will Reflect Christ's Glory

"When Christ, who is your life, appears, then you also will appear with him in glory" (Col. 3:4). Our lives remain a mass of contradictions. This is true of every Christian. We love Christ, but we feel the pull of the world, the flesh, and the Devil. We trust Christ, but we struggle with many doubts and fears. We have new life in Christ, but at the same time our bodies are subject to sickness, aging, and death.

Christians are a mass of contradictions, but it will not always be so. Your love for Christ will be complete, your faith will be turned to sight, and you will experience the joys of everlasting life in a resurrected body. You will be with Christ in glory forever.

Not only will you be in Christ's glory, but his glory will be in you. Paul says, "I consider that our present sufferings are not worth comparing with the glory that will be revealed in us" (Rom. 8:18). Your Christian life is like a tree in winter. It looks bare, but it is alive; and when the spring comes, it will flourish. Its full glory is still to be seen.

Learning to anticipate your future glory is of great benefit in the Christian life. We must use this truth to our advantage when it seems that everything is against us. That's what Paul did: "Therefore we do not lose heart. . . . For our light and momentary troubles are achieving for us an eternal glory that far outweighs them all" (2 Cor. 4:16–17). The apostle is telling us from his own experience how to make sure that we don't lose heart.

God works through the debilitating trials of your life to form a unique reflection of Christ in you that will endure for his glory and to your joy forever. On that day, all that God promises will be ours:

1) We will fully reflect the image and likeness of God.
2) We will be delivered from the curse of evil.
3) We will share the joy of eternal life with redeemed people from all nations.
4) We will enter the presence of God redeemed by the blood of Jesus.
5) We will live this life under the blessing of Christ's rule in his kingdom forever.
6) We will love God with all our heart, soul, mind, and strength, and we will love our neighbor as ourselves.
7) We will rejoice forever in this new life from the grave that is ours through Jesus Christ our Lord.

Consummation: We Will See God

"Then I saw a new heaven and a new earth, for the first heaven and the first earth had passed away, and there was no longer any sea" (Rev. 21:1). John saw a new heaven and a new earth—not a different earth, but a new earth. This earth will finally be redeemed from the curse and liberated from its bondage to decay (Rom. 8:21).

Then John saw "the Holy City, the new Jerusalem, coming down out of heaven from God" (Rev. 21:2). The city has gates facing north, south, east, and west, indicating that God has fulfilled his promise to gather a vast community of people from every nation on earth and to bring them into the joys of life in his everlasting kingdom.

One picture is never enough to capture the glory of what Christ has prepared for us. So alongside the city, John sees the image of a bride beautifully dressed for her husband (Rev. 21:2). Christ is the center of heaven's joy, and all our joy will be in him.

John heard a loud voice from heaven's throne saying, "Now the dwelling of God is with men, and he will live with them. They will be his people, and God himself will be with them and be their God" (Rev. 21:3). Everything that separates us from God is gone. God shares eternal life with all his redeemed people.

God will wipe away every tear from your eyes. Sorrow will be beyond the experience of God's people. There will be no more death or mourning or crying or pain.

Conclusion

God has made amazing promises that only God could deliver. They are fulfilled in Jesus Christ, the Word made flesh. These promises include regeneration, union with Christ, justification, adoption, sanctification, glorification, and the promise of everlasting joy in the consummation of God's redeeming purpose.

All this belongs to those who are in Jesus Christ. It can be yours. The promise is for you and for your children and for all who are far off. Repent. Believe in the Lord Jesus Christ. By believing you will have life in his name (John 20:31).

Notes

1. John Calvin, *The Institutes of the Christian Religion*, 2.12.3 (http://www.ccel.org/ccel/calvin/institutes.iv.xiii.html).
2. Martin Luther, "The Freedom of a Christian," in *Martin Luther: Selections from His Writings*, ed. John Dillenberger (New York: Anchor, 1962), 60.
3. J. C. Ryle, *Holiness* (repr., Chicago: Moody, 2010), 58–59.
4. Owen's original wording is cited by Ryle, *Holiness*, 76–77.

The Gospel Coalition

The Gospel Coalition is a fellowship of evangelical churches deeply committed to renewing our faith in the gospel of Christ and to reforming our ministry practices to conform fully to the Scriptures. We have become deeply concerned about some movements within traditional evangelicalism that seem to be diminishing the church's life and leading us away from our historic beliefs and practices. On the one hand, we are troubled by the idolatry of personal consumerism and the politicization of faith; on the other hand, we are distressed by the unchallenged acceptance of theological and moral relativism. These movements have led to the easy abandonment of both biblical truth and the transformed living mandated by our historic faith. We not only hear of these influences; we see their effects. We have committed ourselves to invigorating churches with new hope and compelling joy based on the promises received by grace alone through faith alone in Christ alone.

We believe that in many evangelical churches a deep and broad consensus exists regarding the truths of the gospel. Yet we often see the celebration of our union with Christ replaced by the age-old attractions of power and affluence or by monastic retreats into ritual, liturgy, and sacrament. What replaces the gospel will never promote a mission-hearted faith anchored in enduring truth working itself out in unashamed discipleship eager to stand the tests of kingdom calling and sacrifice. We desire to advance along the King's highway, always aiming to provide gospel advocacy, encouragement, and education so that current- and next-generation church leaders are better equipped to fuel their ministries with principles and practices that glorify the Savior and do good to those for whom he shed his life's blood.

We want to generate a unified effort among all peoples—an effort that is zealous to honor Christ and multiply his disciples, joining in a true coalition for Jesus. Such a biblically grounded and united mission is the only enduring future for the church. This reality compels us to stand with others who are stirred by the conviction that the mercy of God in Jesus Christ is our only hope of eternal salvation. We desire to champion this gospel with clarity, compassion, courage, and joy—gladly linking hearts with fellow believers across denominational, ethnic, and class lines.

Our desire is to serve the church we love by inviting all of our brothers and sisters to join us in an effort to renew the contemporary church in the ancient gospel of Christ so that we truly speak and live for him in a way that clearly communicates to our age. We intend to do this through the ordinary means of his grace: prayer, the ministry of the Word, baptism and the Lord's Supper, and the fellowship of the saints. We yearn to work with all who, in addition to embracing the confession and vision set out here, seek the lordship of Christ over the whole of life with unabashed hope in the power of the Holy Spirit to transform individuals, communities, and cultures.